INTERNATIONAL CENTRE FOR MECHANICAL SCIENCES

COURSES AND LECTURES - No. 114

ARNOŠT VESELÝ
MEDICAL CYBERNETICS RESEARCH GROUP UHKT, PRAGUE

IGOR VAJDA
CZECHOSLOVAK ACADEMY OF SCIENCES, PRAGUE

# LINEAR ADAPTIVE DECISION FUNCTIONS AND THEIR APPLICATION TO CLINICAL DECISION

COURSE HELD AT THE DEPARTMENT
FOR AUTOMATION AND INFORMATION
JUNE - JULY 1971

Springer-Verlag Wien GmbH 1971

This work is subject to copyright.

All rights are reserved,

whether the whole or part of the material is concerned

specifically those of translation, reprinting, re-use of illustrations,

broadcasting, reproduction by photocopying machine

or similar means, and storage in data banks.

© 1972 by Springer-Verlag Wien
Originally published by Springer-Verlag Wien-New York in 1972

ISBN 978-3-211-81222-8     ISBN 978-3-7091-2876-3 (eBook)
DOI 10.1007/978-3-7091-2876-3

*PREFACE*

*This lecture deals with the application of linear methods of pattern recognition theory to clinical, particularly diagnostic decision. Vector of symptoms (symptomcomplex) measured in a patient represents a pattern, that is necessary to be fit into one of the possible diagnostic classes. The knowledge a priori accumulated by medical science combined with the possible application of adaptive (trainable) clinical decision algorithms provide the best conditions for the use of computers in clinical practice as well as in clinical research.*

*It should be emphasized in the beginning that clinical decision differs in some regards from the current standard classification of geometrical patterns. First of all, the empirical evidence at our disposal does not suggest that the symptomcomplex (considered as a random vector defined by a statistical ensemble of patients) is distributed according to some of the standard parametric distributions. Therefore simple statistical methods based on parameters estimation cannot be used.*

*Another particularly is associated with the really obtainable range of empirical evidence. A standard symptomcomplex is composed of hundreds binary components. Hence, with regards to what was said in the preceding paragraph, it is necessary to esti-*

mate $2^{100} - 2^{1000}$ parameters for the determination of
information usable for adaptation forms as a rule a
thousand, or in the best case a few thousands empirical symptomcomplexes. (That depends on concrete conditions under which the data are collected at clinics).
This means that there is relatively very low ratio
between the range of procurable empirical evidence
and the dimension (informativeness) of the patterns
in the clinical situation we have considered. This
characteristic feature should be taken into account
when the choice of clinical adaptive procedure is
being made.

  Let us characterize briefly the content of the following chapters. Chap. 1, 2 present a
general statistical approach to the theory of adaptive decision functions. Wald's decision model is defined there and within its frame Bayes' optimum decision is introduced. Further, within the frame of
the same model, the concept of general adaptive decision function is defined and asymptotic optimality
and suboptimality of these functions is introduced.

  In Chap. 3 there is the interpretation of a general model, as referred to in Chap. 1,
2 within the framework of clinical situations of the
following three types: a) prognostic, b) therepeutic,
c) diagnostic decision.

  Chap. 4 is concerned in three concrete
types of linear adaptive decision functions, which
appear to be usable in diagnostic decision from both

*the theoretical point of view. These are in certain way modified adaptive functions known from the literature, called here Steinbuch, Bayes and stochastic-approximation functions. Each of these adaptive functions contains free optional parameters by means of which its properties can be modified and optimized.*

*In Chap. 5 a computer program for experimentation with the adaptive functions of Chap. 4 on the basis of concrete clinical data is described briefly. The program has been worked out in the Cybernetics research group of UHKT in Prague*

*Udine, July 1971*

## 1. General decision model

**1.1.** In practice we are often forced to propose effective a l g o r i t h m of decision, without having a desirable description of the s i t u a t i o n, into which such an algorithm should be fitted, at our disposal. As the set of possible decisions is known in advance, incomplete description of the situation can result from  a) the lack of sufficient knowledge about the information source which comes into the input of a system realizing the decision algorithm, or  b) the lack of knowledge about the mechanism that ascribes losses to the individual decision (in some cases both simultaneously).

It is not possible to chose without a good knowledge of situation from the class of a priori procurable algorithms the effective one - yet the notion of optimum is relative with regard to a situation. Effectiveness, respectively the degree of optimality generally changes while changing situation.

**1.2.** The process of accumulating information on situation in order to achieve the optimal decision algorithm is usually called  l e a r n i n g. The learning is an inductive gnoseologic process which begins with collecting empirical data and finishes by formulation of hypothesis about the situation in which the decision algorithm is to work [1].

The learning is sometimes completed before we are going to face the problem of choosing optimal algorithm. In many cases the empirical evidence does not provide plausible relevant hypothesis, i.e. algorithm must be chosen on the basis of incomplete preliminary information. In the course of action of such a suboptimal algorithm a new information appears which is reasonable to be used for subsequent modification and optimization of the algorithm. This information can be represented in various ways, e.g. by the sequence of inputs, or by the sequence of losses caused by previous decisions etc.

When the algorithm is able to utilize information increments for subsequent self-modification step by step we speak about a self-learning or a d a p t i v e  d e c i s i o n algorithm. (*)

1.3. By decision algorithm we will mean throughout this lecture any rule that prescribes certain response to each of the possible inputs. In other words, by decision algo-

---

(*) The adaptive algorithm is an example of cybernetic system with a goal seaking behaviour. The goal, however, does not necessarily have to be the minimum loss attainable after N steps, when $N \to \infty$. Such restrictions as the complexity of realization as well as other ones discussed in §§ 2.4, 4.3, 4.4 below, are usually taken into consideration.

rithm we mean a function and, consequently, in what follows we shall speak about a d e c i s i o n  f u n c t i o n  rather than about a decision algorithm.

Let the possible inputs be elements of the Euclidean n-dimensional space and let $D = \{d^1, d^2, \ldots, d^k\}$ be the set of decision at our disposal. Then the decision function $\delta$ is mapping $E_n \to D$ i.e. $\delta(\underline{x}) \in D$ for $\underline{x} = (x_1, \ldots, x_n) \in E_n$.

The quality of individual decisions $\delta(\underline{x})$ may generally depend on some abstract parameter $\vartheta \in \Omega$, which is not observable directly, i.e. which does not appear in the input of the system realizing $\delta$. In accordance with the classical Wald's [2] model, the following two assumptions are made:

a) that quality of decisions $\delta(\underline{x}) = d \in D$ can be expressed numerically as $L(\vartheta, d)$ independently of $\delta$ and $\underline{x}$. It is supposed that the function $L(\vartheta, d)$ is non-negative on $\Omega \otimes D$, which allows us to interpret the value $L(\vartheta, d)$ as a l o s s  suffered by the decision when the true value of the unknown parameter is $\vartheta$.

b) that there exists a statistical linkage between $\vartheta$ and $\underline{x}$, expressed by a j o i n t  p r o b a b i l i t y  d i s t r i b u t i o n  P of $(\vartheta, \underline{x})$ on $\Omega \otimes E_n$. In other words, we suppose here that $(\vartheta, \underline{x})$ is a pair of random variables (*) with

---

(*)It would be more convenient to differ these random variables from their sample values $(\vartheta, \underline{x})$, e.g. by notation $(\Theta, X)$ - we are not going to do that though.

sample space $E_n$.

As to P, by $P(\Omega^* \otimes E_n^*)$ the probability of the random event $(\vartheta \in \Omega^*, \underline{x} \in E_n^*)$ is denoted, where $\Omega^*$, $E_n^*$ are subsets of $\Omega$, $E_n$. We suppose that it is defined on the product $\sigma$-algebra $\mathcal{S} \otimes B_n$, where $\mathcal{S}$ is an arbitrary $\sigma$-algebra of subsets of $\Omega$, and $B_n$ the Borel $\sigma$-algebra of subsets of $E_n$. The distribution P can be defined by an a priori distribution $P_*$ of the parameter $\vartheta$, defined on $\mathcal{S}$, and by conditional distributions $\{P_\vartheta\}$, $\vartheta \in \Omega$, of $\underline{x}$ given $\vartheta$, defined on $B_n$. Mutual relations between P and $P_*$, $P_\vartheta$ are expressed by the following formulas

$$(1.3.1) \quad P(\Omega^* \otimes E_n^*) = \int_{\Omega^*} P_\vartheta(E_n^*) dP_* \qquad \Omega^* \in \mathcal{S}, E_n^* \in B_n$$

$$(1.3.2) \quad P_*(\Omega^*) = P(\Omega^* \otimes E_n) \qquad \Omega^* \in \mathcal{S}.$$

$P_*$ represents a priori information about $\vartheta$, based on the knowledge of the distribution P only. If sample value $\underline{x}$ becomes known we shall gain a posteriori information about $\vartheta$, represented by a posteriori distribution $P_{\underline{x}}$ of random variable $\vartheta$. Parametric family $\{P_{\underline{x}}\}$, $\underline{x} \in E$, is defined on $\mathcal{S}$ by the following analogue of (1.3.1):

$$(1.3.3) \quad P(\Omega^* \otimes E_n^*) = \int_{E_n} P_{\underline{x}}(\Omega^*) dP^* \qquad \Omega^* \in \mathcal{S}, E_n^* \in B_n.$$

$P^*$ here denotes the marginal distribution of P on $B_n$, defined by

$$P^*(E_n^*) = P(\Omega \otimes E_n^*) \qquad E_n^* \in B_n. \qquad (1.3.4)$$

According to $P^*$ the random variable $\underline{x}$ is unconditionally distributed.

If $\vartheta$ and $\underline{x}$ were statistically independent, then $P = P_* \otimes P^*$ and vice versa.

The average amount of **information** contained in $\underline{x}$ concerning $\vartheta$ is usually measured by Kullback-Laibler's [3] logaritmic measure of divergence between the actual joint distribution $P$ and hypothetical "independent" distribution $P_* \otimes P^*$,

$$I(\vartheta, \underline{x}) = \iint_{\Omega \; E_n} f\left[\frac{dP}{d(P_* \otimes P^*)}\right] dP_* \, dP^*, \qquad (1.3.5)$$

where $f(u) = u \log u$. The derivative in the brackets here denotes the Radon-Nikodym density of $P$ with respect to $P_* \otimes P^*$. If this density does not exist, we put $I(\vartheta, \underline{x}) = +\infty$.

Under some conditions $I(\vartheta, \underline{x})$ can be equivalently defined by

$$I(\vartheta, \underline{x}) = H(P_*) - \int_{E_n} H(P_{\underline{x}}) dP^* = H(P_*) - EH(P_{\underline{x}}) \qquad (1.3.6)$$

where $H(P_*)$ is the a priori entropy and $EH(P_{\underline{x}})$ the average a posteriori entropy of the random variable $\vartheta$. The information can be interpreted as a numerical measure of strength of dependence between $\vartheta$ and $\underline{x}$, $I(\vartheta, \underline{x}) = 0$ if $\vartheta$ and $\underline{x}$ are independent.

1.4 Thus the general model of statistical decision is defined by the following five objects: $\Omega, E_n, D, L(\Omega, d)$,

P) . A special role in our exposition will play the so-called d i s c r e t e  m o d e l (in symbols, $DM(\Omega, \mathcal{E}_n, P)$ ). Here it is supposed $D = \Omega = \{\vartheta^1, \vartheta^2, \ldots, \vartheta^k\}$, i.e. the identification problem is here considered, $d^i = \vartheta^i$. Moreover it is supposed $L(\vartheta^i, \vartheta^j) = 0$ or $1$ depending on whether $i = j$ or not, and

(1.4.1) $\qquad P_\vartheta(\mathcal{E}_n) = 1 \qquad \vartheta \in \Omega,$

where $\mathcal{E}_n$ is the set of all vectors $\underline{x} = (x_1, x_2, \ldots, x_n)$ with binary components $x_i = 0$ or $1$.

When we shall write in the sequel $(\Omega, \mathcal{E}_n, D, L(\vartheta, d), P)$ we shall mean the general model but with P such that the corresponding conditional distributions satisfy (1.4.1).

In the framework of $DM(\Omega, \mathcal{E}_n, P)$ as well as $(\Omega, \mathcal{E}_n, D, L(\vartheta, d), P)$ we will use the following notation

(1.4.2) $p(\vartheta) = P_*(\{\vartheta\}), p_\vartheta(\underline{x}) = P_\vartheta(\{\underline{x}\}), p_{\underline{x}}(\vartheta) = P_{\underline{x}}(\{\vartheta\}), p(\underline{x}) = P^*(\{\underline{x}\})$

for every $\vartheta \in \Omega$ and $\mathcal{E}_n$. According to (1.3.1) or (1.3.3) it holds

(1.4.3) $\quad P(\{\vartheta\} \otimes \{\underline{x}\}) = p(\vartheta) p_\vartheta(\underline{x}) = p_{\underline{x}}(\vartheta) p(\underline{x}) = P(\vartheta, \underline{x}).$

Thus, in $DM(\Omega, \mathcal{E}_n, P)$, the P can be defined either by the distributions $\{p(\cdot), p_\vartheta(\cdot)\}, \vartheta \in \Omega$ or by $\{p_{\underline{x}}(\cdot), p(\cdot)\}, \underline{x} \in \mathcal{E}$. The information (1.3.5) in this special model reduces to

$$\sum_{\vartheta\in\Omega}\sum_{\underline{x}\in\mathcal{E}_n} p(\vartheta) p_\vartheta(\underline{x}) \log \frac{p_\vartheta(\underline{x})}{p(\underline{x})}$$

and (1.3.6) holds provided we put

$$H(P_*) = H\bigl(p(\vartheta^1), \ldots, p(\vartheta^k)\bigr) = -\sum_{\vartheta\in\Omega} p(\vartheta) \log p(\vartheta).$$

1.5. A question arises, how to characterize the quality of individual decision functions $\delta$ within the frame of $(\Omega, \mathcal{E}_n, D, L(\vartheta,d), P)$. In accordance with the classical statistical approach [2], we shall measure this quality by averaging the losses suffered by sample pairs $(\vartheta, \delta(\underline{x}))$,

$$R(\delta) = \iint_{\Omega\ \mathcal{E}_n} L(\vartheta, \delta(\underline{x})) \, dP = E L(\vartheta, \delta(\underline{x})). \qquad (1.5.1)$$

The quantity $R(\delta)$ will be called a r i s k corresponding to $\delta$. In particular, in $(\Omega, \mathcal{E}_n, D, L(\vartheta,d), P)$ it holds

$$R(\delta) = \sum_{\vartheta\in\Omega}\sum_{\underline{x}\in\mathcal{E}_n} L(\vartheta, \delta(\underline{x})) p(\vartheta) p_\vartheta(\underline{x}).$$

The $R(\delta)$ in the frame of $DM(\Omega, \mathcal{E}_n, P)$ can be interpreted as the average probability of incorrect decision by means of $\delta$, because in this case it is easy to see that

$$R(\delta) = \sum_{\vartheta\in\Omega} p(\vartheta)\bigl[1 - P(\delta^{-1}(\vartheta))\bigr] = \text{Probability}\bigl[\delta(\underline{x}) \neq \vartheta\bigr] \qquad (1.5.2)$$

The decision function $\delta_p$ which minimizes the risk is considered as optimum and called B a y e s' d e c i s i o n f u n c t i o n (with regards to P), i.e.

(1.5.3) $$R(\delta_p) = \min_\delta R(\delta) = R_p.$$

The minimum attainable level of risk denoted here by $R_p$ will be called B a y e s' r i s k in the sequel.

Rewriting $R(\delta)$ into the following form

$$R(\delta) = \int_{E_n} \left[ \int_\Omega L(\vartheta, \delta(\underline{x})) \, dP_{\underline{x}} \right] dP^*$$

one can easily see that if we put $\delta(\underline{x}) = d^i$, for $d^i \in D$ satisfying the condition

(1.5.4) $$\int_\Omega L(\vartheta, d^i) \, dP_{\underline{x}} = \min_{d \in D} \int_\Omega L(\vartheta, d) \, dP_{\underline{x}},$$

then $R(\delta') \geq R(\delta)$ for any decision function $\delta'$, i.e. $\delta = \delta_p$. Thus $\delta_p$ always exists and its value $\delta_p(\underline{x}) = d^i$ can be determined by (1.5.4), for every $\underline{x} \in E_n$.

1.6. On the basis of the results stated for example in [4] it can be proved, that in the frame of $DM(\Omega, \mathcal{E}_n, P)$ there exists a reverse relation between $R_p$ and $I(\vartheta, \underline{x})$ : the more complex the information, the lower $R_p$.

The exposition of this chapter can be summarised in the following way. We are interested in decision situations, which can be mathematically described by the five following symbols $(\Omega, E_n, D, L(\vartheta, d), P)$. The problem is to find out Bayes' solution $\delta_p$.

## 2. Adaptive decision functions

2.1. In actual situations we meet in practice just empirical evidence is quite often sufficient for the determination of all five objects mentioned above, but it does not necessarily have to be always like that. Without a doubt is the knowledge of sample space $E_n$ (or in special cases $\mathcal{E}_n$) and decision space $D$. As to the remaining three symbols, various combinations can be imagined. As far as we know the following combinations of objects, which were suggested to be known a priori, have been studied in the literature:

$$(\Omega, E, D, L(\vartheta,d), \{P_\vartheta\}, \vartheta \in \Omega) \qquad (2.1.1)$$

$$(E_n, D) \qquad (2.1.2)$$

$$DM(\Omega, \mathcal{E}_n) \qquad (2.1.3)$$

In the case of (2.1.1) the knowledge of the distribution $P_*$ of $\vartheta$ is missing, in (2.1.2) $(\Omega, L(\vartheta,d), P)$ are missing and in (2.1.3) $P$ is missing. In none of these cases the distributions $\{P_{\underline{x}}\}, \underline{x} \in E_n$ can be specified a priori. Consequently, $\delta_p$ cannot be specified by (1.5.4), too.

In all the reported cases, however, we can approach the optimum decision $\delta_p(\underline{x})$ in certain asymptotic sense, by means of a d a p t i v e   d e c i s i o n   f u n c t i o n s (ADF).

The model in which ADF can be defined requires that the problem of Chap. 1 to adopt the decision $\delta_p(x)$ independently repeats itself many times, each time with the same $(\Omega, E_n, D, L(\vartheta,d), P)$, even partly unknown, but not necessarily with the same values of $(\vartheta, x)$.

Let $(\vartheta_1, x_1), (\vartheta_2, x_2), \ldots$ be the sequence of independent realizations of the pair $(\vartheta, x)$ in the step $i = 1, 2, \ldots$

In other words, let $(\vartheta_i, x_i)$, $i = 1, 2, \ldots$ be a sequence of mutually independent random pairs identically distributed by P. If $d_1, d_2, \ldots$ is a sequence of decisions subsequently adopted according to an arbitrary decision rule, we shall use the following notation: $L_i = L(\vartheta_i, d_i)$, $i = 1, 2, \ldots$,

$$(2.1.4) \quad \Im_n = \begin{bmatrix} \vartheta_1, \vartheta_2, \ldots, \vartheta_N \\ x_1, x_2, \ldots, x_N \\ d_1, d_2, \ldots, d_N \\ L_1, L_2, \ldots, L_N \end{bmatrix} \quad N = 1, 2, \ldots$$

By $I_N$ we shall denote an ordered subset of $\Im_N$. The $I_N$ will be interpreted as the information which is at the disposal in the $(N+1)$-st step(*), when a decision $d_{N+1}$ is to be made on the

---

(*) Besides $I_N$ and $x_{N+1}$, the apriori information represented by the objects in (3.1.1)- (3.1.3) is at the disposal in the $(N+1)$-st step, but this information will not be mentioned explicitly in the sequel.

basis of $\underline{x}_{N+1}$.

General ADF can be defined as a sequence $\Delta = \{\delta_N(\underline{x}|I_{N-1})\}$, $N = 1, 2, \ldots$ of decision functions, $\delta_N(\underline{x}|I_{N-1}) \in D$. Since $I_0$ was not defined, by $\delta_1(\underline{x})$ we shall mean the decision function in the sense of § 1.3.

2.2 The risk $R_N(\Delta|I_{N-1})$ corresponding to ADF $\Delta$ in the Nth step can be measured by

$$R_N(\Delta|I_{N-1}) = \iint_{\Omega\,E_n} L(\vartheta, \delta_N(\underline{x}|I_{N-1})) dP = EL(\vartheta, \delta_N(\underline{x}|I_{N-1})), \quad (2\,2.1)$$

where the expectation $E$ is taken with respect to the pair of random variables $(\vartheta, \underline{x})$.

If some ADF $\Delta$ is given, then the values $d_i$ (and consequently also $L_i$) are completely determined by $\vartheta_1, \underline{x}_1, \ldots, \vartheta_i, \underline{x}_i$. Therefore $I_N$ as a random vector is at given $\Delta$ distributed according to a distribution which is merely depending on the distribution $P$ of $(\vartheta_i, \underline{x}_i)$. The same holds as to the random variable $R_N(\Delta|I_{N-1})$, $N = 1, 2, \ldots$.

Asymptotic optimality of ADF can be defined in different ways.

E.g. we can require (for all possible $P$)

$$\lim_N R_N(\Delta|I_{N-1}) = R_P \quad (2.2.2)$$

or we can require the following condition which is weaker provided $L(\vartheta, d)$ is bounded (*)

(*) See the Lebesgue bounded convergence theorem.

$$(2.2.3) \qquad \lim_N E R_N(\Delta | I_{N-1}) = R_p,$$

where the expectation is taken with respect to $I_{N-1}$. Or, finally, we can require

$$(2.2.4) \qquad \lim_N \frac{1}{N} \sum_{i=1}^{N} L(\vartheta_i, \delta_i(\underline{x}_i | I_{i-1})) = R_p \qquad a.p.[P].$$

If ADF is not asymptotically optimal in certain sense, we say that in that sense it is asymptotically suboptimal.

Adaptation (learning) is stopped at such N, when the risk on the left hand side in (2.2.2) - (2.2.4) is sufficiently close to $R_p$ value. For such N, $\delta(\cdot | I_{N-1})$ is considered to be a suitable approximation of unknown $\delta_p(\cdot)$.

2.3. In the literature on mathematical statistics, pattern recognition and self-learning systems, many asymptotically optimal and suboptimal ADF have been introduced. They are based on different types of $I_N$ within particular problems (2.1.1) - (2.1.3) respectively. In more details they have been or will be dealt with by other lecturers of this summer school. We are going to mention some of them in order to illustrate general concepts introduced above.

In mathematical and statistical literature the case (2.1.1) has been extensively studied. For example A. Špaček [5] proved (for $\Omega = \{\vartheta^1, \vartheta^2\}$) that $\Delta^{(0)}$ based on $I_N^{(0)} = (\vartheta_1,$

$\vartheta_2,\ldots,\vartheta_N) \subset \mathfrak{I}_N$ exists which is optimum in the sense (2.2.2). H. Robbins [6] found (for $\Omega = \{\vartheta^1, \vartheta^2, \ldots, \vartheta^k\}$) necessary and sufficient conditions under which $\Delta^{(1)}$ based on $I_N^{(1)} = (\underline{x}_1, \underline{x}_2,\ldots,\underline{x}_N) \subset \mathfrak{I}_N$ exists which is asymptotically optimum in the sense (2.2.3).

(2.1.2) case have been studied e.g. by B. Shubert [7] who under weak additional conditions proved that $\Delta^{(2)}$ based on $I_N^{(2)} = (I_N^{(1)}, d_1, \ldots, d_N, L_1, \ldots, L_N) \subset \mathfrak{I}_N$ exists, which is asymptotically optimum in a sense close to (2.2.4).

We are going to deal with the case (2.1.3), extensively studied in the domain of system sciences, in the sequel and therefore as an illustration we only mention ADF $\Delta^{(3)}$ based on $I_N^{(3)} = (I_N^{(0)}, I_N^{(1)}) \subset \mathfrak{I}_N$ and working in accordance with the nearest neighbor principle. T. Cover and P. Hart [8] found in the case $\Omega = D = \{\vartheta^i,\ldots,\vartheta^k\}$ and $L(\vartheta^i, \vartheta^j) = 0$ or 1 depending on wether $i = j$ or $i \neq j$ the following estimate of the left hand side expression $R_p^*$ in (2.2.4):

$$R_p \leq R_p^* \leq R_p\left(2 - \frac{kR_p}{k-1}\right).$$

In other words, for small values of the probability of error $R_p =$ = Probability $[\delta(\underline{x}) \neq \vartheta]$, $\Delta^{(3)}$ is close to the asymptotic optimality.

2.4. The case (2.1.3) which is in question in pattern recognition theory and practise seems to be very simple from the theoretical point of view. For the sake of simplicity let us restrict our attention to $DM(\Omega, \mathcal{E}_n, P)$. Denote by $\hat{p}^N(\vartheta)$, $\hat{p}^N_\vartheta(\underline{x})$ the relative - frequency estimates of $p(\vartheta)$, $p_\vartheta(\underline{x})$ based on the information

$$\hat{I}_N = I_N^{(3)} = (\vartheta_1, \ldots, \vartheta_N, \underline{x}_1, \ldots, \underline{x}_N), \quad \vartheta \in \Omega, \quad \underline{x} \in \mathcal{E}_n.$$

Thus, in general, $k \cdot 2^N - 1$ parameters are estimated (see § 1.4).

It follows from the strong law of large numbers that

$$(2.4.1) \quad \lim_N \hat{p}^N = p(\vartheta), \lim_N \hat{p}^N_\vartheta(\underline{x}) = p_\vartheta(\underline{x}), \text{a.s.}[P], \vartheta \in \Omega, \underline{x} \in \mathcal{E}_n.$$

If we put $\hat{P}_N(\vartheta, \underline{x}) = \hat{p}^N(\vartheta) \hat{p}^N_\vartheta(\underline{x})$, (1.4.3) and (2.4.1) will imply

$$(2.4.2) \quad \lim_N \hat{P}_N(\vartheta, \underline{x}) = P(\vartheta, \underline{x}) \quad \text{a.s.}[P],$$

for every $\vartheta \in \Omega$, $\underline{x} \in \mathcal{E}_n$.

Thus, if we define $\hat{\Delta} = \{\delta_N(\cdot \mid I_{N-1})\}$, $N = 1, 2, \ldots$ by

$$(2.4.3) \quad \delta_N(\underline{x} \mid \hat{I}_{N-1}) = \delta_{\hat{P}_{N-1}}(\underline{x}), \quad \underline{x} \in \mathcal{E}_n,$$

then ARF $\hat{\Delta}$ is obviously asymptotically optimum in the sense (2.2.2).

In order to understand why the simple $\hat{\Delta}$ is often inapplicable in the pattern recognition practise we must notice for which N (2.2.2) warrants that $R_N(\hat{\Delta}|\hat{I}_{N-1}) = R(\delta_{\hat{P}_{N-1}})$ will be most likely close to $R_p = R(\delta_p)$. Altogether $k \cdot 2^N - 1$ parameters are to be estimated. It means that if we can suppose nothing about P (or at least $\{P_\vartheta\}, \vartheta \in \Omega$) a priori, then the necessary sample size N must be of order at least $k \cdot 2^N$. The number of population k is not too large in the practice but, as we said above, in diagnostic decision (as well as many other situations) we are faced with $100 \leq N \leq 1000$. In these caes purely mathematical solution, based on the limits in § 2.2 fails.

The last conclusion may not seem well-founded. An objection may arise why not use, for maximum really obtainable N, ARF $\hat{\Delta}$. But, as it has been proved by Gilbert's [9] experiments, this is not maximum we can do for decreasing $R(\delta_N)$ for really attainable N and this approach could be misleading. In the experiments, for $\Omega = \{\vartheta^1, \vartheta^2\}$, general families of distributions $\{P_\vartheta\}$ on $\mathcal{E}_n$ have been examined. It was shown that, for realtively small N, the risks $R(\delta_{\hat{P}_N})$ are quite higher than $R(\delta_N)$ for $\delta_N$ from such ARF $\Delta$, which evidently is not asymptotically optimum. About these results we are going to report in § 4.4. in more details.

What we have just said can explain the existence of a large number of ADF for pattern recognition. It is evident more or less at first sight, that most of these ADF are asymptotically optimum only under very special conditions, practically nonverifiable. This concerns all linear methods, in particular those we are going to mention later. Applicability of such ADF is decided on the basis of empiria. If the sample values of $R(\delta_N)$ obtained from a control ensamble of pairs $(\vartheta_i, \underline{x}_i)$ are satisfactory (for a concrete unknown $P$), the ADF or the $\delta_N$ is considered as applicable.

2.5. In this as well as in the following sections we shall restrict to the (2.1.3) model (*), bearing in mind only those ADF, which are based on $\hat{I}_N = I_N^{(3)}$ information. Under these assumptions usually linear ADF (LADF) are used in practice. Before defining them we shall introduce a concept of automaton ADF (AADF).

Suppose that a mapping $\delta : \mathcal{E}_n \to \Omega = D = \{\vartheta^1, \ldots, \vartheta^k\}$ depends on a vector parameter $\underline{a} = (a_1, a_2, \ldots, a_m) \in E_m$, i.e. $\delta(\underline{x}) = \delta(\underline{x}|\underline{a})$ and let $\gamma : (\Omega \otimes \mathcal{E}_n \otimes E_m) \to E_m$ be an arbitrary transformation. Then input set $\Omega \otimes \mathcal{E}_n$, output set $D$, set of inner states $E_m$, initial state $\underline{a}_0$, and the transformations $\delta, \gamma$, define some automaton. Each automaton of this structure defines ARF $\{\delta_N\}$, $N = 1, 2, \ldots$ by

---

(*) The restriction to DM in (2.1.3) is not essential. All the following concepts can be introduced even in the frame of general model $(\Omega, E_n, D, L(\vartheta, d), P)$ when the knowledge of $P$ is lacking and ADF based on $\hat{I}_N$ are used.

$$\delta_1(\underline{x}) = \delta(\underline{x}|\underline{a}_0),\ \delta_2(\underline{x}) = \delta(\underline{x}|\underline{a}_1),\ \ldots,\ \delta_N = \delta(\underline{x}|\underline{a}_{N-1}),\ \ldots$$

where (2.5.1)

$$\underline{a}_i = \gamma(\vartheta_i, \underline{x}_i, \underline{a}_{i-1}),\quad i = 1, 2, \ldots \qquad (2.5.2)$$

is the inner state of the automata after the i-th output $\delta_i(\underline{x}_i) = \delta(\underline{x}_i|\underline{a}_{i-1})$ has been realized. Thus the automata we have considered here are that of Mealy.

The advantage of AADF as compared with general ADF is that instead of the sequence $I_N$ of increasing length, the memory of AADF is charged by a fixed number $m$ of components of $\underline{a}_N$ for any $N = 1, 2, \ldots$ .

By LADF in this lecture such AADF denoted, for which $\underline{a} = (w_1, \ldots, w_{1n}, w_{21}, \ldots, w_{kn}) \in E_{kn}$, and there exists a function $F: E_k \to D$ such that $\delta(\underline{x}|\underline{a}) = F((\underline{x}, \underline{w}_1), \ldots, (\underline{x}, \underline{w}_k))$, where $\underline{w}_i = (w_{i1}, \ldots, w_{in})$. The scalar products $(\underline{x}, \underline{w}_i)$ as arguments of $\delta$ are motivating the term "linear" in LADF.

In the following, the components of $\underline{a}$ will be recorded into an $n \times k$ matrix $W = [\underline{w}_1, \underline{w}_2, \ldots, \underline{w}_k]$ with columns $\underline{w}$, i.e.

$$W = \begin{bmatrix} w_{11} & w_{21} & \ldots & w_{k1} \\ w_{12} & w_{22} & \ldots & w_{k2} \\ \ldots & \ldots & \ldots & \ldots \\ w_{1n} & w_{2n} & \ldots & w_{kn} \end{bmatrix}, \qquad (2.5.3)$$

and $\delta(\underline{x}|W)$ will be written instead of $\delta(\underline{x}|\underline{a})$. Similarly $\gamma(\vartheta,\underline{x},W)$ will stand in the place of $\gamma(\vartheta,\underline{x},\underline{a})$. Note that no restriction is posed on the form of $\gamma(\vartheta,\underline{x},W)$.

All the LADF we shall deal with in this lecture will have the function $F(x_1,x_2,\ldots,x_k)$ defining $\delta(\underline{x}|W)$ of the following form: $F(x_1,x_2,\ldots,x_k) = \vartheta^i \in D$ iff

$$(2.5.4) \qquad x_i \geq \max_j x_j + \nu,$$

where $\nu \geq 0$ is a constant.

## 3. Clinical decision

3.1. In the end of Chap. 1 the Bayes' solution $\delta_p$ of the decision problem $(\Omega, E_n, D, L(\vartheta,d), P)$ have been defined. In Chap. 2 we have explained how a suitable approximation of $\delta_p$ by means of $\delta_N(\cdot) = \delta_N(\cdot|I_{N-1})$ can be obtained, provided the distribution $P$ is not a priori known to us. In this chapter we are intended to interpret the abstract objects in $(\Omega, E_n, D, L(\vartheta,d), P)$ in the framework of clinical decision situations.

In clinical practice one can distinguish prognostic, therapeutic and diagnostic decision. The prognostic decision include prognosis of the further course of the disease in the patient, when the disease is going to finish, the type of invalidity may outlast and so on. The therapeutic decision is to provide the best possible therapeutic procedure for the patient. The d i a g n o s t i c decision is to identify the patient's disease.

Parameter $\vartheta \in \Omega$ in all three cases represents the state of the patient. The sample $\underline{x}$ represents all information at our disposal about the patient's state. The information includes patient's anamnestic data, the result of clinical tests and assays, etc. As the greatest part of components $x_i$ of $\underline{x}$ represents the presence or absence of certain symptoms (which is encoded by 1 or 0 respectively), we shall suppose, for the sake of simplicity, that all the information about patient is encoded by means of symbols 0, 1, i.e. that $\underline{x} \in \mathcal{E}_n$ is a binary-components vector. Human statistical ensamble defines the distribution P of the pair $\vartheta, \underline{x}$, conditional distributions $P_\vartheta$, a priori distribution $P_*$ etc. The interpretation of $\Omega, \mathcal{E}_n, P$ given here is common for all clinical decision situations. As to the interpretation of D and $L(\vartheta, d)$, it depends on which of the three decision situations defined above we bear in mind. We are going to describe it in the following three sections.

3.2. The elements of the decision space $D = \{d^1, d^2, \ldots, d^k\}$ in prognostic decision represent individual types of vocational or personal invalidity of the patient after the treatment, then lasting or temporary pathological consequences of certain types of deseases and so on. All these cases are concerned in a decision about the fact that the patient's state $\vartheta(t)$ is going to belong into certain subset $\Omega^* \subset \Omega, \Omega^* \in \mathcal{J}$ after a time $t > 0$. Thus the particular types of invalidity, pathological consequences etc. define a system $\{\Omega^1, \Omega^2, \ldots, \Omega^k\}$ of mutually disjoint subsets of $\Omega$ in such a manner that $d^i$ can be identified with $\Omega^i$.

With $\vartheta(t)$ a random symptomcomplex sample $\underline{x}(t)$ is statistically associated. $\vartheta(t)$ as well as $\underline{x}(t)$ depend on the type of treatement which is based on the information $\underline{x} = \underline{x}(0)$ about the patient which is at disposal at present time $t = 0$. Hence the optimality of prognostic decision functions $\delta: \xi_n \to D$ should be defined with respect to a definite (e.g. standard) treatement. But another approach is possible too, namely, the treatement (as well as diagnosis etc.) can be encoded by means of a binary sequence and by this sequence $\underline{x}$ can be extended. This, however, gives to rise up rather complicated feedback system which has not been really applied as far as we can say.

The prognostic decision function $\delta: \xi_n \to D$ itself is convenient to be considered as a convolution $\delta_* \delta^*$, where $\delta_*: \xi_n \to \xi_n$ is a predictor of $\underline{x}(t)$ using the information $\underline{x}(0)$ and $\delta^*: \xi_n \to D$ defines proper prognostic decisions on the basis of predictions $\underline{x}(t)$. Therefore the convolution is to be understood as follows: $\delta(\underline{x}) = \delta^*(\delta_*(\underline{x}))$. Note that $\delta_*$ represents prognosis in the sense of the word and adaptation in situation where $P$ is unknown is concerned mainly in this predictor.

It does not seem reasonable to interpret the loss $L(\vartheta, d)$ for $\vartheta = \vartheta(0)$ directly. In the prognostic decision situation one can expect that rather than $L(\vartheta, d)$ losses $\ell(d^i, d^j)$, caused by a prognostic decision $d^i$ provided $\vartheta(t) \in \Omega^i$, can be numerically estimated. But even in this situation the framework of Wald's model can be formally reached. At $\vartheta = \vartheta(0), \underline{x} = \underline{x}(0)$ is distributed by $P_{\vartheta(0)}$. The application of standard treatment defines for every $\underline{x}$ a conditional distribution $Q_{\underline{x}}$ of the state $\vartheta(t)$ on $\mathcal{Y}$. Define $\lambda(\vartheta(t), d) = \ell(d^i, d)$ for $\vartheta(t) \in \Omega^i, d \in \Omega$ so that

$$\lambda : \bigcup_{i=k}^{k} \Omega^i \circ D \to E_1 .$$

Since, clearly,

$$Q_{\underline{x}}\left(\bigcup_{i=1}^{k} \Omega^i\right) = 1 \quad \text{for every } \underline{x},$$

we can define

$$L(\vartheta(0), d) = \iint_{\mathcal{E}_n \Omega} \lambda(\vartheta(t), d) \, dQ_{\underline{x}} \, dP_{\vartheta(0)} = \sum_{\underline{x} \in \mathcal{E}_n} \int_{\Omega} \lambda(\vartheta(t), d) \, dQ_{\underline{x}} P_{\vartheta(0)}(\underline{x}) =$$

$$= \sum_{\underline{x} \in \mathcal{E}_n} \sum_{i=1}^{k} \ell(d^i, d) \, Q_{\underline{x}}(\Omega^i) P_{\vartheta(0)}(\underline{x}).$$

The average value $L(\vartheta, d)$ defined by this manner seems to be a reasonable measure of losses when the actual present state of the patient is $\vartheta(0) = \vartheta$ and the prognosis is $d \in D$.

3.3. In therapeutic decision $D = \{d^1, d^2, ..., d^k\}$ represents the therapies that are at disposal and $L(\vartheta, d)$ losses resulting from a therapy $d \in D$ provided the patient's actual state is $\vartheta \in \Omega$.

$L(\vartheta, d)$ do not have to have mere interpretation as the effectiveness of therapies, but it also may include for example pains con nected with the application of the therapy, the expense of the therapy, time necessary for the treatment as well as the risks of side-effects in patients etc.

Here the following important clinical problem arises. Let $\tilde{\Omega} = \{\Omega^1, \Omega^2, \ldots, \Omega^k\}$ be an arbitrary decomposition of $\Omega$, write $\vartheta^i$ instead of $\Omega^i$ and define

(3.3.1) $$L(\vartheta^i, d) = \sup_{\vartheta \in \vartheta^i} L(\vartheta, d)$$

Let us define further probability distribution $\tilde{P}$ on $\tilde{\Omega} \otimes \mathcal{E}_n$ by (see § 1.4):

$$\tilde{P}(\vartheta^i, \underline{x}) = \int_{\vartheta^i} P_\vartheta(\underline{x}) \, dP_* \quad \text{for every } \vartheta^i \in \Omega, \underline{x} \in \mathcal{E}_n.$$

$\tilde{P}$ together with (3.3.2) define a new decision problem $(\Omega, \mathcal{E}_n, D, L(\vartheta^i, d), \tilde{P})$. The problem first suggested by A. Perez [10, 11] consists in finding of such $\vartheta^i \subset \Omega$ providing minimum difference between Bayes risk $R_p$ of the original problem and Bayes risk $R_{\tilde{p}}$ of the new decision problem. In fact, that is a problem of optimum choice of diagnoses $\vartheta^i$ with regards to an a priori given set of possible therapies $D$. It is not known whether the current diagnostic classification of possible patient states into diseases satisfies such an optimality criterion or not.

Ledley [12] has considered therapeutic decision model $(\Omega, \mathcal{E}_n, D, L(\vartheta, d), P)$ with finite $\Omega$ in the situation (2.1.1), where $P_*$ is unknown. Therefore Bayes solution $\delta_p$ cannot be determined. Ledley suggests that in such a situation minimax decision function $\delta_0$ should be used which is defined by (cf. § 1.4).

$$\min_{\delta} \max_{\vartheta} \sum_{\underline{x} \in \mathcal{E}_n} L(\vartheta, \delta(\underline{x})) p_\vartheta(\underline{x}) = \max_{\vartheta} \sum_{\underline{x} \in \mathcal{E}_n} L(\vartheta, \delta_0(\underline{x})) p_\vartheta(\underline{x}).$$

It holds $\delta_0 = \delta_P$ iff $R_P \geq R_{\tilde{P}}$ for every $\tilde{P}$ such that $\tilde{P}_\vartheta = P_\vartheta$, $\vartheta \in \Omega$, i.e. iff $P_*$ is the least favourable a priori distribution, maximizing $L_P$ under the given $\{P_\vartheta\}$, $\vartheta \in \Omega$.

3.4 In the diagnostic decision it is supposed that there is a finite number of diagnosis and the aim is to identify them (see [12, 13]). Therefore we shall put $\Omega = D = \{\vartheta^1, \vartheta^2, \ldots, \vartheta^k\}$, where $\vartheta^i$ is interpreted as the i-th diagnosis. Remark that $\Omega$ does not have to mean the class of all possible diagnosis (e.g. accordingly to the nomenclature of World Health Organization) but only diagnosis concerning, for example, diseases of certain organ, or it can be $\Omega = [\vartheta^1, \vartheta^2]$ only, where $\vartheta^1$ means "patient is healthy" and $\vartheta^2$ means "patient is ill" etc. The losses are reasonable to be defined here by the relation

$$L(\vartheta^i, \vartheta^j) = \begin{cases} 0 & \text{for } i = j \\ 1 & \text{for } i \neq j \end{cases} \quad \text{cf. [12]} \quad (3.4.1)$$

so that $R(\delta) = \text{Prob}[\delta(\underline{x}) \neq \vartheta]$ (see § 1.5), i.e. we can say that $R(\delta)$ is a probability that the actual diagnosis $\vartheta$ will differ from the established one $\delta(\underline{x})$. Similarly $R_p$ can be interpreted as a minimum attainable probability of error. Since the distribution P of $(\vartheta, \underline{x})$ is usually not known in the practice, we see that $DM(\Omega, \mathcal{E}_n, P)$ in the situation (2.1.3) is the realistic mathematical model for diagnostic decision. This somewhat differs from the initial approach to clinical diagnostic decision in [13]

### 4. LADF for diagnostic decision

4.1. In this and the following chapter we shall consider $DM(\Omega, \mathcal{E}_n, P)$ defined in § 1.4 in the situation (2.1.3). Moreover we shall suppose $P_\vartheta[x_n = 1] = 1$ for all $\vartheta \in \Omega$. When the latter requirement cannot be guaranteed, another coordinate $x_{n+1}$ identically equal 1 is supposed to be added and $\mathcal{E}_n$ replaced by $\mathcal{E}_{n+1}$.

In this section a special LADF will be defined, it will be called S t e i n b u c h ' s LADF and it will be denoted by $S(\mu, \nu)$. It is called Steinbuch's LADF because the rule for changing internal state matrix W is similar to that at Steinbuch's learning matrices [14]. It is a certain generalization of LADF described by Nilsson [15] on page 87. The function $\delta(\underline{x}|W)$ is defined by the following condition

(4.1.1) $\delta(\underline{x}|W) = \vartheta^i$ if $(\underline{x}, \underline{w}_i) \geq \max_{j \neq i} (\underline{x}, \underline{w}_j) + \nu$.

When such $i$ does not exist, the decision is not accepted resp. decision $\vartheta^0$ is accepted by which the space $\Omega = D$ can be extended. The function $\gamma(\vartheta, \underline{x}, W)$ (rule of reinforcement of weights) is defined by the following condition

$$\gamma\left(\vartheta^i, \underline{x}, [\underline{w}_1, \ldots, \underline{w}_k]\right) = \begin{cases} [\underline{w}_1, \ldots, \underline{w}_i + \mu\underline{x}, \ldots, \underline{w}_k] \\ \quad \text{when } \delta(\underline{x}|W) \in \{\vartheta^i, \vartheta^0\} \\ \\ [\underline{w}_1, \ldots, \underline{w}_j - \underline{x}, \ldots, \underline{w}_i + \underline{x}, \ldots, \underline{w}_k] \\ \quad \text{when } \delta(\underline{x}|W) = \vartheta^j \notin \{\vartheta^i, \vartheta^0\} \end{cases} \quad (4.1.2)$$

When this rule is modified in the following way:

$$\gamma\left(\vartheta^i, \underline{x}, [\underline{w}_1, \ldots, \underline{w}_k]\right) = \begin{cases} [\underline{w}_1, \ldots, \underline{w}_i + \mu\underline{x}, \ldots, \underline{w}_k] \\ \quad \text{when } \delta(\underline{x}|W) = \vartheta^i \\ \\ [\underline{w}_1, \ldots, \underline{w}_i + \underline{x}, \ldots, \underline{w}_i + \underline{x}, \ldots, \underline{w}_k] \\ \quad \text{when } \delta(\underline{x}|W) = \vartheta^0 \\ \\ [\underline{w}_1, \ldots, \underline{w}_j - \underline{x}, \ldots, \underline{w}_i + \underline{x}, \ldots, \underline{w}_k] \\ \quad \text{when } \delta(\underline{x}|W) \notin \{\vartheta^i, \vartheta^0\} \end{cases}$$

then we speak about $S_1(\mu, \nu)$. $\quad (4.1.3)$

It is evident, that in $S(\mu,\nu)$ value $\delta(\underline{x}|W) = \vartheta^0$ is concieved as correct decision whereas in $S_1(\mu,\nu)$ as incorrect one. In fact in both cases $\vartheta^0$ is a fictive decision only without any factual interpretation and if $\delta(\underline{x}|W) = \vartheta^0$ the actual decision has to be made in another way than by means of LADF.

It follows immediately from the definition, that $S(\mu,\nu), S_1(\mu,\nu)$ should be considered for $\mu \in [0,1], \nu \in [0,+\infty)$ only. Initial weights of matrix W are assumed to be equal to zero.

In the case of $k = 2$ parameter $\mu$ in formula for

weights reinforcement was used firstly by Butz [16]. Parameter represents a "zone of uncertainty" and the thought of using the zone appeared in [17]. It was demonstrated there on concrete clinical data that the relation between the number of incorrectly classified $\underline{x}$ (i.e. between $P[\delta(\underline{x}) \neq \vartheta]$ and $P[\delta(\underline{x}) = \vartheta^0]$) changes in accordance with curves of the following type

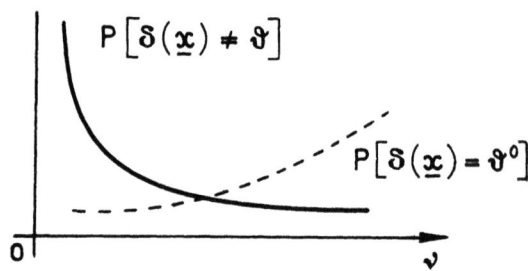

In literature beginning with Rosenblatt's [18] perceptron LADF similar to Steibuch's LADF are mostly considered, especially $S(0,0) = S_1(0,0)$.

Imperfections of $S(\mu,\nu), S_1(\mu,\nu)$ are obvious. Except for some special linear separable cases, for which convergence theorem can be proved (see p. 87 in [15]), it is impossible to expect, that these ADF will satisfy some of the conditions (2.2.2) - (2.2.4). But for properly chosen $\mu,\nu$ these methods may give very satisfactory results in many real situations.

4.2 Bayesian LADF denoted by $B(\nu)$ is defined according to the following rule

$$\delta(\underline{x} \mid W) = \begin{cases} \vartheta^i & (\underline{x}, \underline{w}_i) \geq \max_{j \neq i} (\underline{x}, \underline{w}_j) + \nu \\ \vartheta^0 & \text{if such } i \text{ does not exist} \end{cases} \quad (4.2.1)$$

The rule $\gamma(\vartheta, \underline{x}, W)$ for sequential change of weights of matrix $W$ will not be explicitly described here because of its very complicated form. There are given expressions for weights in the N-th step only, $N = 1, 2, \ldots$

$$w_{ij} = \log \frac{\hat{P}_{\vartheta^i}[x_j = 1]}{1 - \hat{P}_{\vartheta^i}[x_j = 1]} \quad j = 1, 2, \ldots, n-1, \quad (4.2.2)$$

$$w_{in} = \sum_{j=1}^{n-1} \log \hat{p}(\vartheta^i)(1 - \hat{P}_{\vartheta^i}[x_j = 1]). \quad (4.2.3)$$

Here

$$\hat{P}_{\vartheta^i}[x_j = 1] = \frac{N_{ij} + 1}{N_i + 2}, \quad \hat{p}(\vartheta^i) = \frac{N_i + 1}{N + 2}, \quad (4.2.4)$$

where $N_{ij}$ is frequency of those $\underline{x}$ in the sequence $\underline{x}_1, \underline{x}_2, \ldots, \underline{x}_{N-1}$, for which $x_j = 1$ and simultaneously $\vartheta_\ell = \vartheta^i$, while $N_i$ is the frequency of $\vartheta_\ell = \vartheta^i$ in the sequence $\vartheta_1, \vartheta_2, \ldots, \vartheta_{N-1}$.

The first expression (4.2.4) was suggested by Good [19] as an estimator of unknown conditional probability $P_{\vartheta^i}[x_j = 1]$. This estimator differs from classical one by additive constants 1 and 2, which guarantee that $B(\nu)$ will be defined also for $N=1$ or for those $N$'s, for which $N_i = 0$. The second expression in (4.2.4) is an analogical frequency-estimator of unknown a priori probability $P_*(\vartheta^i) = p(\vartheta^i)$.

If components $x_i$ of $\underline{x}$ are statistically independ ent for each $\vartheta \in \Omega$ (this hypothesis will be denoted by $\mathcal{H}$). it was shown by Minsky [20] that $B(0)$ turns into $\hat{\Delta}$ (see § 2.4)

If hypothesis $\mathcal{H}$ is valid and W is defined according to (4.2.2), (4.2.3), and if, moreover, $\hat{P}_{\vartheta^i}[x_i=1] = P_{\vartheta^i}[x_i=1]$, then $\delta(\underline{x}|W) = \delta_p$, i.e. (4.2.1) is optimal decision function. As (4.2.4) and the law of large numbers imply under $\mathcal{H}$

$$\lim_N \hat{P}_{\vartheta^i}[x_i=1] = P_{\vartheta^i}[x_i=1] \quad \text{a.s.} \quad [P]$$

$\hat{\Delta} = B(0)$ is asymptotically optimal (in the sense of (2.2.2)).

It is obvious, that $\mathcal{H}$ is not generally true and therefore in general $B(\nu)$ is asymptotically suboptimal. But it will be shown in § 4.4, that for really obtainable N the probability of error of suboptimal $B(0)$ is lower than that of optimal $\hat{\Delta}$. This is caused by the fact, that in the contrary to $k \cdot 2^N - 1$ parameters in case of $\hat{\Delta}$, only $k \cdot N - 1$ parameters $p(\vartheta^i)$, $i=1, 2, \ldots, k-1$, $P_{\vartheta^i}[x_j=1]$, $j=1,2,\ldots,k$, $i=1,2,\ldots,k$ are estimated in case of $B(0)$ (in both cases all estimators are based on $\hat{I}_{N-1}$). An estimation of $k \cdot N - 1$ parameters for k equal approximately to tens and n to hundreds is really attainable, while an estimation of $k \cdot 2^N - 1$ parameters is not. It is possible to decrease the probability of error by means of proper choice of parameter $\nu$ independently on validity of $\mathcal{H}$.

4.3. Stochastic-approximation LADF, denoted by $SA(\nu)$, is defined by (4.2.1) and by the following rule for reinforcement of weights (see [21]):

$$\gamma(\vartheta, \underline{x}, [\underline{w}_1, \ldots, \underline{w}_k]) = [\underline{w}'_1, \ldots, \underline{w}'_k],$$

where

$$\underline{w}'_i = \underline{w}_i - \frac{x}{N}[\chi_i(\vartheta) - (\underline{w}_i, \underline{x})]. \qquad (4.3.1)$$

Here $N = 1, 2, \ldots$ denotes the number of reinforcement step and $\chi_i(\vartheta) = 1$ or $-1$ for $\vartheta = \vartheta^i$ or $\vartheta \neq \vartheta^i$ respectively. It is evident that $SA(\nu)$ is not AADF exactly in the sense of § 2.5, because function $\gamma$ depends on $N$. It is still automaton, but in this case the one with time variable structure, as far as the change of in ternal state (reinforcement) is concerned. It is well-known (see [21]) that $SA(0)$ is ADF for which $\delta_N$ minimizes a quality measure similar to the probability of error $P[\delta_P(\underline{x}) \neq \vartheta]$ as $N$ approaches infinity, provided $\{P_\vartheta\}$ satisfy certain strict conditions.

4.4. It will be shown in this section on the basis of Gilbert's interesting results which is the relation between optimality of $B(\nu)$ and optimality of asymptotically optimum ADF $\hat{\Delta}$ (see § 2.4 and the end of § 4.3).

In mentioned Gilbert's paper it was supposed that $k = 2$, $\Omega = \{0, 1\}$, $n = 7$ (where $x_7 = 1$ independently on $\vartheta = 0$ or $\vartheta = 1$), $p(0) = p(1) = \frac{1}{2}$,

$$p_\vartheta(x_1, \ldots, x_6) = \exp\left[\alpha + \sum_{i=1}^{7} \alpha_i (-1)^{y_i} + \sum_{i<j} \alpha_{ij} (-1)^{y_i + y_j}\right].$$

where $\alpha_i, \alpha_{ij}$ are free optional parameters, common to all distributions $\{P_\vartheta\}$, $\vartheta \in \Omega$, $y_i = x_i$ for $i = 1, 2, \ldots, 6$, $y_7 = \vartheta$.
The $\alpha_{ij}$ are regulating mutual dependence between $x_i$ and $x_j$ for $i \neq j$.

The first experiment consists in a concrete choice of parameters $\alpha_i, \alpha_{ij}$ and in a realization of $\hat{I}_N = I_N^{(3)} = ((\vartheta_1, \underline{x}), (\vartheta_2, \underline{x}_2), \ldots, (\vartheta_N, \underline{x}_N))$ for $N = 100$. Typical results for 5 different groups of parameters $\alpha_i, \alpha_{ij}$ are given in the following table.

| Risk | Experiments | | | | |
|---|---|---|---|---|---|
| | 1 | 2 | 3 | 4 | 5 |
| $R(\delta_p) = R_p$ | 0,1766 | 0,1156 | 0,0721 | 0,2542 | 0,1152 |
| $R_{101}(\hat{\Delta} \mid I_{100})$ | 0,2609 | 0,1676 | 0,1239 | 0,3405 | 0,1920 |
| $R_{101}(B(0) \mid I_{100})$ | 0,1766 | 0,1172 | 0,0737 | 0,2580 | 0,1172 |

It can be seen, that $R_N(B(0) \mid \hat{I}_{N-1})$ is closer to $R_p$ than $R_N(\hat{\Delta} \mid \hat{I}_{N-1})$ in all the five cases.

The second experiment differed from the first one in choice of $N = 500$ only. It follows from a table given further that the difference between $R_N(\hat{\Delta} \mid \hat{I}_{N-1})$ and $R_N(B(0) \hat{I}_{N-1})$ are smaller than in the first experiment, but LADF $B(0)$ is still better than asymptotically optimal ADF $\hat{\Delta}$. At the same time it is necessary to consider, that $n = 7$ is relatively small in comparison with $n$ which equals similarly to hundreds in diagnostic decision problems.

| Risk | Experiments | | | | |
|---|---|---|---|---|---|
| | 1 | 2 | 3 | 4 | 5 |
| $R(\delta_P) = R_P$ | 0,1766 | 0,1156 | 0,0721 | 0,2542 | 0,1152 |
| $R_{501}(\hat{\Delta} \mid I_{500})$ | 0,1856 | 0,1352 | 0,0892 | 0,2841 | 0,1317 |
| $R_{501}(B(0) \mid I_{500})$ | 0,1766 | 0,1172 | 0,0737 | 0,2580 | 0,1172 |

## 5. Computer program for LADF

5.1. In Chap. 3 $DM(\Omega, \mathcal{E}_n, P)$ has been interpreted as a mathematical model of clinical diagnostic decision. It was supposed that $\Omega, \mathcal{E}_n$ are only known. In Chap. 4 we have reported some concrete LADF $\Delta$ solving the experience decision problem arising here.

From the discussion of these $\Delta$ we can see the following. If in practice we are to face an actual diagnostic problem, we shall not be able to decide without $P$ which of the $\Delta$ is the best one. Therefore in any such case we shall have to accumulate the information $\hat{I}_{N-1} = I_{N-1}^{(3)}$ composed of by realizations $(\vartheta_i, \underline{x}_i)$ of $(\vartheta_i, \underline{x})$. The sample $(\vartheta_i, \underline{x}_i)$ is supposed to be provided by the i-th patient of an appropriate statistical ensemble of patients. Using this information we can form $\delta_N(\cdot \mid I_{N-1})$ for every $\Delta$ under considerations $(\vartheta_N, \underline{x}), \ldots, (\vartheta_{N+K}, \underline{x}_{N+K})$, we can estimate $R\,\delta_N(\cdot \mid \hat{I}_{N-1}) = R_N(\Delta \mid \hat{I}_{N-1})$ by the following relative frequency of errors:

$$(5.1.1) \qquad \frac{1}{k+1} \sum_{i=0}^{k} L\left(\vartheta_{N+i}, \delta_N\left(\underline{x}_{N+i} \mid \hat{I}_{N-1}\right)\right).$$

By the law of large numbers (5.1.1) converges with $k \to \infty$ to $R_N(\Delta \mid \hat{I}_{N-1})$ a.s. [P]. Comparing the empirical effectiveness (5.1.1) for all $\Delta$ under consideration, the best LADF can be chosen.

It is quite possible that the best LADF for one ensemble of patients (i.e. for one P or one diagnostic decision problem) may be entirely unacceptable for other ensemble. It is also possible that few of the LADF $\Delta$ may exhibit approximately identical good results. In a similar case all the LADF can be applied simultaneously and the decision of one of them can be tested by decisions of others.

5.2. For the above mentioned reasons we have realized a computer program that enables to compare the empirical effectiveness of the LADF under consideration. The program is therefore able to realize $\delta_N(\cdot \mid \hat{I}_{N-1})$ and to verify the effectiveness for $\Delta = S(\mu,\nu), S_1(\mu,\nu), B(\nu)$ and $SA(\nu)$ and for free optional values $\mu \in [0,1]$, $\nu \in [0,+\infty)$.

In the program a statistical ensemble S composed by realizations $(\vartheta'_1, \underline{x}'_1), \ldots, (\vartheta'_M, \underline{x}'_M)$ of $(\vartheta, \underline{x})$ corresponding to M patients is supposed to be at our disposal. The ensemble is randomly decomposed into two disjoint subensembles $S_1, S_2$ containing $M_1, M_2$ realizations respectively, $M_1 + M_2 = M$. Then $(\vartheta_1, \underline{x}_1), \ldots,$

# Computer Program

$(\vartheta_{N-1}, \underline{x}_{N-1})$ is carried out by means of a generator of pseudo-random numbers $j = 1, 2, \ldots, M_1$ by the following way: if in the i-th step the generators produces $1 \leq j \leq M_1$, we put $(\vartheta_i, \underline{x}_i) = (\vartheta'_j, \underline{x}'_j) \in S_1$. Using this procedure possible effects of artificial ordering of the samples in $S_1$ are eliminated and N greater than relatively small $M_1$ can be investigated. Similarly $(\vartheta_N, \underline{x}_N), \ldots, (\vartheta_{N+K}, \underline{x}_{N+K})$ are produced, with $S_1$ replaced by $S_2$.

Using the information $\hat{I}_{N-1} = ((\vartheta_1, \underline{x}_1), \ldots, (\vartheta_{N-1}, \underline{x}_{N-1}))$ the program produces $\delta_N(\cdot | I_{N-1})$ for $N = N_\ell$, $\ell = 1, 2, \ldots$, where $1 \leq N_1 < N_2 < \ldots < N_m$ are specified in advance. For every $N = N_\ell$ sequence $(\vartheta_N, \underline{x}_N), \ldots, (\vartheta_{N+K}, \underline{x}_{N+K})$ is generated and the relative frequency (5.1.1) evaluated and printed. With the same $\hat{I}_{N+1}$, $N = 2, 3, \ldots, N_m$, this procedure is subsequently realized for every LADF under consideration.

Then, for every $N_\ell$, $\ell = 1, 2, \ldots, m$, empirical effectivenesses (5.1.1) corresponding to all the LADF are compared. The principle of the program can also be seen from the flow chart.

It should be specified in the program which of the LADF is going to be verified and how $\vartheta$ or $\mu$ are to be specified. Further we must specify integers $k, m, n$ and the sample sizes K and $N_1 < N_2 < \ldots < N_m$.

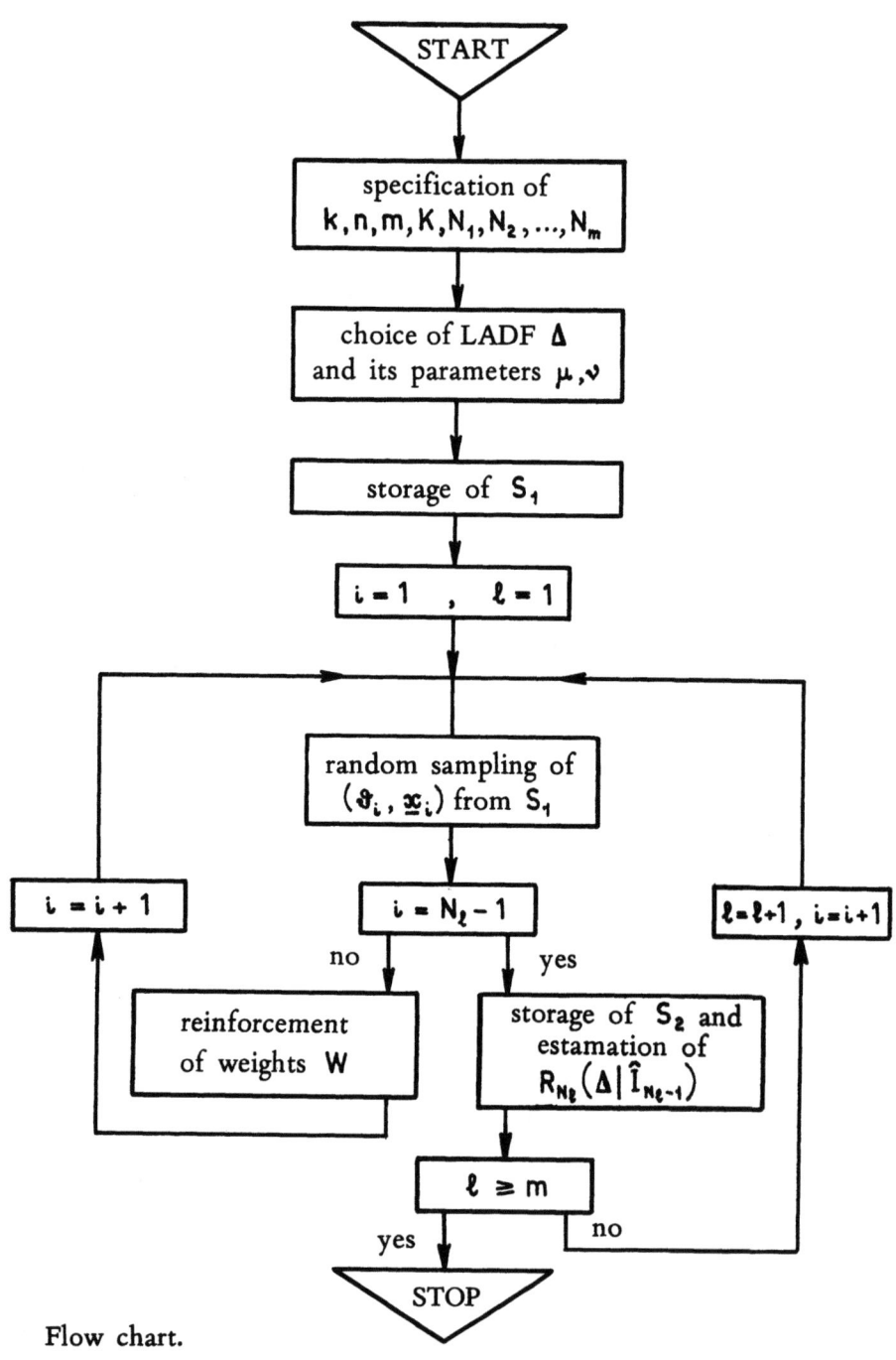

Flow chart.

5.3. Let us add several technical comments on the program. It has been realized in Fortran IV and specified for the computer MINSK 22. The subensembles $S_1$ or $S_2$ are stored bitwiser (one component of $x'_i$ in one bit of the word). Every $x_i$ is stored in five words of the operational storage. Since MINSK 22 computer has 36 - bit words (except the sign bit, which is not used) it is possible to process vectors $x'_i$ of up to 180 components, i.e. $n \leq 180$. The corresponding parameter values $\vartheta'_i$ are stored in a table of pairs $(i, \vartheta'_i)$ in the operational storage.

In order to avoid wasting room in the operational memory, there is always only one of the subensembles i.e. $S_1$ during the adaptation and $S_2$ during the estimation of LADF effectiveness. The one of the subensembles which is not applied in given phase of program is stored in the external storage. As MINSK 22 has got rather limited operational storage (9.046 of 36-bit words) and has no fast external storage (neither disc nor dram storage), our program is capable of processing $S_i$ ensembles for $M_i \leq 500$ (for $n \leq 180$ ).

In case we should like to use the program for a large computer, its adjustment would be rather easy since Fortran IV was used. Its capacity could be extended by means of a simple adjustment, so that essentially higher $k, n$ and $M_i$ could be used.

# REFERENCES

[1] M.S. Watanabe: Knowing and Guessing, Willey, N.Y. 1967

[2] A. Wald: Statistical Decision Functions, Willey N.Y. 1961

[3] S. Kullback, R. Leibler: On information and sufficiency. Ann. Math. Stat. 22 (1951), 79–86.

[4] I. Vajda: A contribution to informational analysis of patterns. In: Methodologies of Pattern Recognition (ed. by M.S. Watanabe), Academic, N.Y. 1969

[5] A. Spacek: An elementary experience problem. Trans. 2nd Prague Conf. on Inf. Theory,..., Prague 1959

[6] H. Robbins: The empirical Bayes approach to statistical decision problems. Ann.Math.Stat. 35 (1964),N.1

[7] B.O.Schubert: Bayesian model of decision making as a result of learning from experience. Ann. Math. Stat. 40 (1969),No.6

[8] T.M. Cover, P.E. Hart: Nearest neighbor pattern classification. IEEE Trans. on IT-13 (1967), 21-27

[9] E.S. Gilbert: On discrimination using qualitative variables. Jour. Amer. Stat. Ass. 63 (1968), No. 324, 1399–1412

[10] A. Perez: Information, −sufficiency and data reduction problems, Kybernetika (Prague) 1 (1965), No. 4

[11] A. Perez: In: Progress of Cybernetics (ed. by J. Rose), Gordon & Breach, London 1970

[12] R. Ledley: Use of computers in Biology and Medicine. McGraw-Hill, New York 1965

[13] R. Ledley, L. Lusted: Reasoning Foundations of Medical Diagnosis Science 130 / 1959 /, 3366, 9-21

[14] K. Steinbuch: Adaptive networks using learning matrices. Kybernetik 2 (1965), 148-152

[15] N. Nilsson: Learning Machines, McGraw, N.Y. 1965

[16] Butz: Perceptron type learning algorithm in nonseparable situations. J.Math.Anal.Appl.17(1967),560-576

[17] A. Vesely : Linear adaptive system for medical diagnosis. Kybernetika (Prague) 7(1971), No. 2

[18] F. Rosenblatt: Principles of Neurodynamics, Spartan Books, W. 1962

[19] I.J. Good: The estimation of probabilities. Res. Monograph 30. Cambridge, Mass., M.I.T. Press 1965

[20] M. Minsky: Steps toward artificial intelligence. Proc. IRE, January 1961, 8-30

[21] J.Z. Cypkin: Foundations of the Theory of Trainable systems (in Russian), Nauka, M. 1970

## CONTENTS

|  | page |
|---|---|
| Preface.................................................... | 3 |
| 1. General Decision Model............................. | 7 |
| 2. Adaptive Decision Functions....................... | 15 |
| 3. Clinical Decision..................................... | 24 |
| 4. LADF for Diagnostic Discussion.................. | 30 |
| 5. Computer Program for LADF...................... | 37 |
| References................................................ | 43 |

MIX
Papier aus verantwortungsvollen Quellen
Paper from responsible sources
FSC® C105338

If you have any concerns about our products,
you can contact us on
**ProductSafety@springernature.com**

In case Publisher is established outside the EU,
the EU authorized representative is:
**Springer Nature Customer Service Center GmbH
Europaplatz 3, 69115 Heidelberg, Germany**

Printed by Libri Plureos GmbH
in Hamburg, Germany